Touched

Ian Marriott

To Christine,
with thanks for all your kindness
and support.
Love
Ian T. Marriott xxx

Cinnamon Press
:: small miracles from distinctive voices ::

Published by Cinnamon Press
Office 49019, PO Box 92, Cardiff, CF11 1NB.
www.cinnamonpress.com

ISBN 978-1-78864-136-4

British Library Cataloguing in Publication Data. A CIP record for this book can be obtained from the British Library.

Designed and typeset in Bodoni by Cinnamon Press. Cover design by Adam Craig.

Cinnamon Press is represented by Inpress Ltd.

Acknowledgements

With thanks to Jan Fortune at Cinnamon Press. And to all at the MBC poetry group, for their continued friendship and critical support.

Contents

To Margaret Gillies Brown

Touched

The Hurting

i

The *abandoned* child

plays and replays
his loop of pain

until in the end
there's little else

a stuck record
ground-hog day

year after year
proofed by itself

play it again

*

Both oppressor
and oppressed—

in a single body
the bully, and abused.

How to unravel
this tangle of selves,

an inner violence
become so great?

Unable to cope
with being one

a man may split
himself in two

the devil forms
his coalition

righteous pitched
against the damned

ii

At first there was only
the mother's flank,

her warm body,
the un-warm world,

until, one evening,
she turned you aside,

falling in space,
frozen in time.

iii

Pond Skater

A Fön wind
from the wrong quarter
upends me—

or the slow dark
of a rising trout.

So perilous
this thin meniscus—

six legs splayed out.

iv

Caught between
the python's coils,

each out-breath
a death grip—

though not, as you'd think,
snake as other,

muscling round
that lost cause—

but *divided self*
throttling its own,

the slow smile
swallows you whole.

*

Or trap-door spider,
assassin under
its silken lid—

burrowing through
the body's bounds,

hapless victim
dragged within.

v

Front leg missing,
one hundred percent dog—

he loped towards us
without an ounce
of self pity—

that whole, un-whole body,
muscled and twisting
against its loss.

vi

The scorpion alone
under its rock,
a whole life
braced for attack—

he will out-last
the human race,
endless state
of high alert—

will never know
the warmth of another,
just searing heat,
this desert frost.

vii

A man zips
his loneliness in a bag

slung over
that cold shoulder

will leave his life
in a flash

viii

The wolves have loped
for three days

to stalk and kill
their shaggy prey

the musk-ox close
their muscled ranks

precious calf
corralled within

ix

A lone tree
hammered hard
by hail and sheep.

There is little here
but rain and wind,

even the weasel traps,
set across their water conduit
are empty.

*

From his green land-rover
the moor-keeper performs
his predatory tasks,

nothing is allowed
above its station,
nothing is allowed—

except the sky,
opening and closing
its chest of colours,

there is little
he can do
to keep out the light.

x

Last night the roof ripped clean off
and we're up in the rafters again—

glass-eyed shark
eating its tail in a feeding frenzy,

or the Sperm whales'
hanging weight.

*

A river dredges
its own estuary,
to keep the sea at bay—

is that the voice of another,
half an ocean away?

xi

Caged in the waters
of a stagnant loch,

and how on earth
did we get to this—

crushed against the flanks of others,
unable to make the real journey,

our very flesh turned against us,
lurid pink from that muscled red—

yet even here
in this writhing madness,

the birth pool calls,
our ancient text.

xii

The sea pours into herself,
the moon performs
its welcome task—

each life an emergence,
crawling up its shingle beach—

or the Catfish,
caught in its own gilled limbo
slipping endlessly from creek to creek.

xiii

The sirens are singing
their strange lament,

out of the wilderness
as you have known,

but a life by the shore
beckons you on,

the warmth of another
thawing these bones.

xiv

Over half a life, never quite
at home on land,

like the Mudskipper,
making its brief wet forays,

until the lungs opened,
great gulping gasps of air,

and the slit-gills lie useless,
re-absorbed into a drying flank.

xv

Storm in a tea-cup
this life-time fetch

a maddening gyre
wholly our own

the whirlpool draws
inward and down

a mind mis-remembers
its decade of pain

glossing completely
your violence and fall.

Old friends
on the ocean dock

the returning world
changed but the same

a deepening keel
steadies me now

there is nothing here
I will not endure

or turn aside
with a trick of the light.

xv

You'd think being touched
was something bad

and so it seemed
in the crazy years

but once the pain
had run its course

a gift bestowed

xvi

In the end it's like
some sort of club

those who survive
their own death

like the awkward gatherings
of war veterans

huddling round
their insular truth

as now I enjoy
the small things most

breakfast croissants
warmed in the oven

the scent of coffee
climbing the walls

or warmth of my dog
in the early morning

knowing nothing and everything
of what is to come

Mangrove

Scratching a living
where others won't,

one foot brackish
one foot not,

you bind this wound
with fresh and salt,

what life there is
within these roots.

Ground Water

Trickling down
through solid rock,
this water rained
before man's fall,

and now it flows
from deep within,
hugging the mountain's
desert flank,

to a secret village
of well-kept terraces,
and the water master
of old Oman,

bent to his task
through ancient rite,
portioning sweetness
to this field, and that—

each life offered
its allotted share,
Allahu Akbar
or nothing at all.

Umbilical

Two days up
we nearly lost our hanging tent,

to wind and darkness,
the terrible wind—

and hardly spoke again,
inching up that granite skin,

twinned as if
within the womb.

*

And why do you do it?
Mallory was asked—

for a few days
of animal knowing,

the joy of a body
at home in itself?

After an ascent of a climb called Zodiac, El Capitan, Yosemite Valley, California, which a friend and I made in late autumn 1994. The climb took 3 days, and being very steep we slept for 2 nights in a hanging 'portaledge' tent. For two days we suffered a terrible windstorm, during which speaking was pretty much useless, and we were reduced to a form of poor man's telepathy for communication. It was a very pure experience.

Migrant

On a Derbyshire hillside
a hundred birders
swivel their scopes,
a collective gasp
as you rise and soar.

Lonely Lammergeyer,
tail shot-through
on the long journey,
how we welcome you
into our fold,

as a hundred walkers
at Samphire Hoe
turn their backs
on the loaded dinghy
flailing offshore.

After Heidegger

Walking upon the open moor
my dog has no eye for a pretty view,
occupied, only, with matters at hand,
the flushing of grouse, scent of a hare,
or whippet in heat
who passed this way three days ago—

and I can only write these words,
the scent of *dwelling* long misplaced,
rhymes of vistas wide and fair,
but not the clay beneath my feet.

Being and Time

It came on slowly
with the passing of friends,

hourglass catching
its own reflection.

A sunset darkens
to *that* starry night,

there is something here
which was not before.

A Poem at Fifty

1

Look! Out to the left a black hole
is chomping its way through the centre of the galaxy—
like a good boy, eating his space-time crust.

2

Mr Cox tells us that space is just
an un-fillable vacuum— like an un-fillable sandwich—
so what is he smiling about!

3

My bones are turning slowly inward,
early beginnings of a fifties sag.

And so to explain this rising happiness—
sticking to the ribs
like an old-wives-tale
of spontaneous combustion,
the body a wick, burning up—

or St. Vitus Dance, which,
(we are led to believe)
can actually happen,
from time to time.

Sand Grouse

It was a hundred miles
to the nearest watering hole
and a hundred back,

yet even this a safer bet
to raising a brood
within the harrier's reach.

So twice daily, he'd trust his clutch
to the dun mother, the desert heat,
and fly for hours, only to sink

his breast into a muddy pool,
then fly back—water laden—
cowering past the talon's stoop.

*

And in late autumn,
the year's offspring fledged and gone,
he withdraws alone

to the deep silence,
from which he, himself,
had come.

Turf

Last week, a pile of builders' rubble,
today, this perfect pitch of green—

how dangerous to live
without a sense of history,

the shallow-rooted
inherit the earth.

Pit Pony

Three thousand years
in the wild Carneddau

three thousand years
of wind in your mane

shackled to industry
the long dark

blinkered and burdened
you shoulder your load

the kindness of miners
easing the pain

memory of hills
branded within

Inveraray, September

A grey heron
hunched on the tide,

shoreline always
a sense of becoming—

day-trippers slip
from city buses,

here to measure
their lives.

Pangolin

The pangolin performs
his Charlie Chaplin walk,

armour-plated from tip-to-toe,
his only line of attack
is defence.

If rumbled, he curls into a tidy ball—
scaly tail right up to his nose,
and is quite impregnable!

On a good day
he can out-fox a whole pride of lions—
booted about like a loose football,

until off he trots, or digs down,
proofed in his own pangolin world.

Butterfly

The butterfly is out, at last—
wings drying
in the mid-day sun,
he becomes a creature of light.

And there was little at all
to hint at this—
darkness grubbing
the cellulose of leaves,

until the chrysalis of pain
grew from within,
liquefaction of self
fixed to a plan—

and he will make good use
of the time that's given,
nettle and Buddleia
his allies now.

Hyphae

Asleep, I sink
beneath the day,

the body sheds
its outer form;

opening into
this private space,

so little here
between us now.

Lightning Source UK Ltd.
Milton Keynes UK
UKHW010117080222
398328UK00002B/196

9 781788 641364